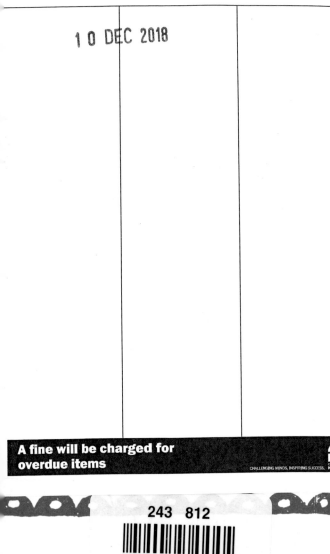

A CARD FROM ANGELA CARTER

A CARD
FROM
ANGELA
CARTER

SUSANNAH CLAPP

B L O O M S B U R Y

LONDON · BERLIN · NEW YORK · SYDNEY

First published in Great Britain 2012

Copyright © 2012 by Susannah Clapp

Endpaper illustration © Corinna Sargood

The moral right of the author has been asserted

Bloomsbury Publishing Plc
50 Bedford Square
London
WC1B 3DP

www.bloomsbury.com

Bloomsbury Publishing, London, Berlin, New York and Sydney
A CIP catalogue record for this book is
available from the British Library

ISBN 978 1 4088 2690 4

10 9 8 7 6 5 4

Typeset by Hewer Text UK Ltd, Edinburgh
Printed in Great Britain by Clays Ltd, St Ives plc

For

Liz Calder, Carmen Callil and Deborah Rogers

– three of Angela's friends

TWENTY YEARS AGO I went for the first time into Angela Carter's study. I knew the rest of her house in Clapham quite well. Downstairs was carnival: true, there was a serious kitchen, but there were also violet and marigold walls, and scarlet paint-work. A kite hung from the ceiling of the sitting room, the shelves supported menageries of wooden animals, books were piled on chairs. Birds – one of them looking like a ginger wig and called Carrot Top – were released from their cages to whirl through the air, balefully watched through the window by the household's salivating cats. 'Free range,' said Angela.

Here Angela's husband Mark Pearce dreamed up the pursuits he went on to master: pottery, archery, kite-making, gunmanship, school-teaching; here friends streamed in and out for suppers; here their son Alexander was a much-hugged child.

The study was unadorned, muted, more fifties than sixties. Not so much carnival as cranial. There was a small wooden desk by the window looking down to the street, The Chase: 'SW4 0NR. It's very easy to remember. SW4. Oliver. North. Reagan.' There was a grey filing cabinet, shabby, well organised and stuffed with papers. I knew some of what I would find in that cabinet – Angela had told me – but there had not been time to go through everything.

She had died a few weeks earlier, on 16 February 1992. She was fifty-one and had been suffering from lung cancer for over a year. Her early death sent her reputation soaring. Her name flew high, like the trapeze-artist heroine of *Nights at the Circus*. Fevvers, the 'Cockney Venus', zoomed upwards, 'shaking out about her those tremendous red and purple pinions, pinions large enough, powerful enough to bear up such a big girl as she. And she was a *big* girl . . . Now all London lies beneath her flying feet.' Three days after she died, Virago sold out of Angela's books. She became, in words from the two poles of her vocabulary, an *aerialiste* and a celeb.

Not that her fiction and her prose went unacknowledged while she was alive. She was not neglected and rarely had anything rejected; she was given solo reviews and launch parties; she went on television; she got cornered by fans. But she was not acclaimed in the way that the number of obituaries might suggest. She was ten years too old and entirely too female to be mentioned routinely alongside Martin Amis, Julian Barnes and Ian McEwan as being a young pillar of British fiction. She was twenty years too young to belong to what she considered the 'alternative pantheon' of Iris Murdoch, Doris Lessing and Muriel Spark in the forties, when 'in a curious way, women formed the ascendancy'. She spoke with some fellow feeling about J. G. Ballard, who was, she correctly predicted, about to be turned by critics from a science-fiction cult figure into a mainstream literary one. 'Ballard is rarely, if ever, mentioned in the same breath, or even the same paragraph as such peers as Anthony Powell or Iris Murdoch. Fans such as Kingsley Amis and Anthony Burgess praise Ballard to the skies, but they themselves are classified differently as, God help us, "serious writers" in comparison.'

We had talked about these things a year earlier, after her illness had been diagnosed and she had asked me to be her literary executor. We had met at the end of the seventies, when I was helping to set up the *London Review of Books* and was keen to get Angela to write for the paper. Liz Calder, who had shortly before published *The Passion of New Eve* and *The Bloody Chamber* at Gollancz, arranged an introduction and, swaddled in a big coat, Angela came into the small office, which had been carved out of the packing department in Dillons bookshop. She lit up the paper's pages for the next twelve years. And we became friends.

Her requirements for her estate were relaxed, if not exactly straightforward: I should do whatever was necessary to 'make money for my boys', for Mark and Alexander. There was to be no holding

4

the same story – the killing of a woman by her teenage daughter and friend – as Peter Jackson's 1994 film *Heavenly Creatures*. Her largest unproduced theatrical work was a version of Wedekind's *Lulu*, a hard (elongated, sprawling) play to bring off, but apt for Angela. She was beguiled by Louise Brooks, who had glided onto celluloid as Lulu. Admiring the challenge her eyes threw out under the famous fringe, Angela claimed that, 'Should I ever have a daughter, I would call her not Simone, not even Rosa but Lulu.' It was imaginative of Richard Eyre's National Theatre to commission the adaptation in 1987, but though the script went through several densely written drafts, it was eventually rejected. Angela was not forgiving. When I ran into her at a party in Tufnell Park shortly afterwards, she was white-faced and narrow-eyed with fury: 'The National have just flushed my *Lulu* down the toilet.' The most tantalising unfinished piece was something she had not mentioned during our talks: a treatment of Virginia Woolf's sex-change novel *Orlando* which she had started to turn into an opera to be set to music by Michael Berkeley.

One of Angela's ideas was that the entire production should take place in the fabric department of Marshall & Snelgrove.

There were other, more personal, unpublished finds. I knew she had drawn but I had not realised how much. Tucked in among the files were richly coloured crayon pictures: of flowers with great tongue-like petals, of slinking cats, and of Alexander, whose baby face with its bugle cheeks, dark curls and big black eyes looked like that of the West Wind on ancient maps; his mother described his face as being like a pearl.

She had told me that she kept journals and described the shape they took. They were partly working notes and partly casual jottings, roughly arranged so that the two kinds of entry were on opposite pages. They were stacked in the study: lined exercise books in which she had started to write during the sixties and which covered nearly thirty years of her life. She decorated their covers as girls used to decorate their school books, with cut-out labels (the Player's cigarette sailor was one), paintings of cherubs and flowers and patterns of leaves.

Inside she described, in her clear, upright, not quite flowing hand 'a smoked gold day' in 1966, and in the same year made a list of different kinds of monkeys: rhesus, capuchin and lion-tailed. She wrote of the 'silver gilt light on Brandon Hill' in 1969, jotted down a recipe for soup using the balls of a cock and, in her later pages, took notes on Ellen Terry's lectures on Shakespeare. She made, again and again, lists of books and lists of films (Jean-Luc Godard featured frequently). She did not write down gossip (though she liked gossip), and wrote little about her friends. She specialised in lyrical natural description and in dark anecdote. She noted that the Danish astronomer Tycho Brahe had died of a burst bladder because he had not dared to get up from a banquet to have a pee. She observed that the pork pies favoured by her mother's family for wakes, in part because they could be bought ready-made, 'possess a semiotic connection with the corpse in the coffin – the meat in the pastry', and added, referring to Beatrix Potter's most chilling tale of fluffy life: 'Tell that to Tom Kitten.' She wondered what smell Alexander would remember from his childhood home.

The revelation for me in the journals was that, in her twenties, Angela had written poems – verses that strikingly prefigured her novels in richness of expression, in their salty relish, in their feminism and in their use of fable. At the same time she produced a statement of intent which came startlingly close to prophesy: 'I want to make images that are personal, sensuous, tender and funny – like the sculpture of Arp, for example, or the paintings of Chagall. I may not be very good yet but I'm young and I work very hard – or fairly hard.'

I have a small collection of Angela material. As well as the newspaper cuttings, the business notes from publishers, the grief-filled letters from friends after her death, there are a few browning, frayed letters, written mostly on lined exercise-book paper, always in longhand (though her hand was square rather than long), generally prompted by some *London Review* inquiry to her when she was abroad. There is on my mantelpiece a clockwork Russian doll, made out of tin with bright orange blotches on her cheeks and a design of blue teardrops on her stiff full skirt: a present from Angela and Mark. And there are a dozen or so cards, dashed off in greeting or explanation, sometimes with a full message, sometimes just a salute. These cards make a paper trail, a zigzag path through the eighties. They are casually despatched – some messages are barely more than a signature – but are often the more telling for that: they catch Angela on the wing, shooting her mouth off. She would have hated the idea of a soundbite, but she had a gift for a capsule phrase, for a story in a word. In their celerity, postcards are the email of the twentieth century, but they are also more than that. They tell more than one story: the photographs, paintings and cartoons that Angela chose sometimes reinforce but often contradict the message on the other side. They can contain hidden histories: some of Angela's images glance back at an episode in her life, or hint at a conversation we had been having. Sometimes, of course, the choice of picture is random: it hints at nothing. In a few years' time it will be harder to know which is random, which is allusive.

I first looked at these cards when writing a series of talks about postcards for Radio 3; I looked at them again when it was suggested to me that those talks might become a book. I look at them now with the idea that they evoke some of the occasions, preoccupations and delights of Angela's life. A life of which, as she put it, 'The fin has come a little early this siècle.'

LIVING DOLLS

Here they are, the girls. Five of them sitting in a row. Some are smaller in girth than others, but all of them have plump curved cheeks, dark almond eyes and slightly open cupid mouths. Each is sumptuously and decorously clad in early twentieth-century mode. All have titfers perched on their heads: one with a lace trim secured by a pearl, another with flowers slipping down its slopes, a third with a fronded plume like a pony's tail. They are done up primly in tightly secured collars, lace bibs and ruffs, and full sleeves. But their stiff legs are wide apart, their long skirts are partly rolled up; you can see petticoats and a flash of drawers.

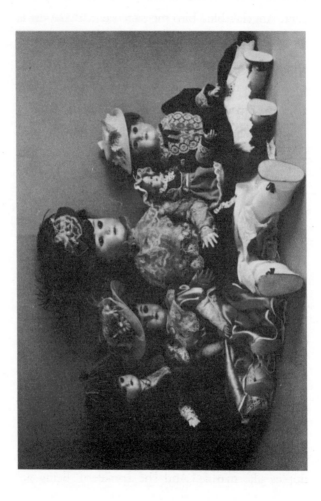

The card, posted in the summer of 1989 from London but bought in Hungary, was nearly not sent. Angela's blue-biro message says: 'Budapest is *bliss, bliss, bliss.* So much so that I never got to post any letters.' She has added in black ink: 'I found this among my souvenirs & thought I'd post it off, anyway.' I'm glad she did. Of the cards I've seen from Angela, certainly of those she sent me, this brown and white, lush but shadowy photograph is the one that most evokes her stories and essays: not her style – the picture is posed, stately, static, striving for correctness, the very opposite of Angela's helter-skelter hoopla prose – but her subject matter. These creatures are dolls – it's hard not to think of *The Magic Toyshop* – whose bodies are too rigid to be saucy and too adult to be petted; they are showcases of femininity, made-up versions of the sex that makes itself up.

Fascinated by pretenders, shams, copies and twins, Angela wrote about the way that leather and suede and velvet can 'simulate the skin it conceals', and the way plaster can be made to look as if it ripples like marble. And she spoke of being an

13

impersonator. As a young journalist, she said she would, 'quite unconsciously, posit a male point of view as the general one. So there was an element of the male impersonator about this young person as she was finding herself.' As a big, pink-skinned and blue-eyed creature in Japan, she looked into the eyes of her dainty dark lover and saw that she had become 'a kind of phoenix, a fabulous beast; I was an outlandish jewel. He found me, I think, inexpressibly exotic. But I often felt like a female impersonator.'

By the time I knew her, Angela's face was free of make-up and her hair stripped of dye. She was the first woman I knew who went grey without looking like a granny: on the contrary, she turned everything on its head by doing so as she was becoming a mother. Her disregard not only for fashion but for neatness was a dirty-strike display. It was not that she was uninterested in people's appearance – on one of the last afternoons I spent with her she went through our acquaintances ranking them in order of handsomeness. Still, she herself stopped putting on the Ritz. Antonia Fraser, appearing on a television programme with Angela, once said that she had not been able to conceal a flicker of astonishment when Angela had admired her dress. No flicker was ever lost on Angela. 'I wonder why people are always so surprised when I'm interested in clothes,' she said, not wondering at all. And laughed. She abandoned fashion with caustic flair and childlike defiance. When Lorna Sage discovered, while staying with her, that she had lost her make-up, Angela handed her a Japanese paintbox, which Sage described as 'some kind of actor's or geisha's kit, which was all slick purple, rusty carmine and green grease'.

Angela had many guises: the only constant feature of being snapped was, she said with some pride, that photographers were always asking her to lower her cheekbones. In her twenties, with short curls, attenuated limbs and a loose scarf round her neck, she looks like a faun and seems to be sitting on a mushroom. The many studies of her in maturity, when she was both heavier and better known, are less whimsical and not often smiling. There was Angela in her last year, at her typewriter, chin on hand, looking fed up, in a capacious plaid skirt and a sloppy joe (perhaps the jumper that Carmen Callil remembers her wearing to Glyndebourne); in front of her – as shorthand for 'writer' – is a big waste-paper basket piled high with papers. There is Angela in headscarf and thin-framed specs looking jolly and forthright and toothy, a rare cast of face that made her look like some media idea of a librarian. There she is in an extraordinary midnight-blue, black and brown Holy Family composition with Mark and Alexander, in which the three of them seem to be travelling out of shadows, with the light hitting only the sides of Mark and Angela's faces and her arm. Alex is perched on his father's shoulders, holding on to his long curls, looking seraphic; Mark is bearded, dark-browed, and looks, for all his steady atheism, like John the Baptist; Angela smiles up at him, holding onto her baby's chubby foot.

Still, the pictures that show her alone in close-up are the most compelling. She had a large but fluid, almost fuzzy face; watching her was sometimes like looking at someone underwater,

Not least because their beautiful seriousness misses out so much. Angela laughed often and loudly. She was a cackler. She was also a talker, a gasser and a tremendous chatterer on the phone. Angela belonged to the radio age, growing up with the sweetness of John Masefield's *Box of Delights* and the sepulchral tones of *The Man in Black*. She claimed that the wireless was 'the most visual of mediums because you cannot see it', and steered her plots through a tremendous range of sounds. The opening moments of her 1976 play *Vampirella* feature the cooing of doves, the scrape of nails against the bars of a cage, a harp that sounds like laughter and the screech of a bat; in her play about the afflicted painter Richard Dadd, broadcast three years later, there are hobgoblin choruses and camel shriekings; in its radio form, *The Company of Wolves* resounds to the rattle of bones and the noise of throat-slitting. She asked for chill, asexual voices, tiny fairy screams and affected coughs. She knew what it was to make a voice distinctive – as a schoolgirl, she had wanted to act – and her own tones were unmistakable.

Piping, soft, with clipped vowels, at times Angela

sounded like a parody of girlish gentility. At other times she skidded into casual south London. You never knew exactly where you were. She was impossible to second-guess. She was a great curser, and took pride in this: 'I am known in my circle as notoriously foul-mouthed.' Yet she was also byzantinely courteous: her most full-blooded protests would often be heralded by an icily disarming 'forgive me', accompanied by a salaam and a chuckle. She surrounded her trenchancies with long pauses, wheezes of silent laughter, verbal flutters. She slithered into some of her sharpest remarks through a series of hesitancies that were a world away from diffidence. What seemed to be an obstruction in her speech could become a weapon. I remember her on a television books panel that had been reverencing D. H. Lawrence. She made as if to speak and then unleashed an extremely long, goose-pimpling pause, the sort of silence that is usually cut from a broadcast. Suddenly she let rip: 'I've always thought that Gudrun was, well, the vasectomy queen of the north.' From the stunned response, you might have thought one of those Hungarian dolls had belched or breathed flame.

CARNIVAL

From St Louis in the late eighties Angela sent a card that flew the flag for her writing. Bill Owens' celebrated photograph of the 1972 Good Times Parade in Pleasanton California is gaudy, comical and at first glance hard to make out. It is a non-posh, popular display – but what exactly is it showing?

In the foreground of the black-and-white picture are two bare-chested middle-aged men, one wearing specs and the other shades. They are flabby and they are grinning. They look a bit proud and a bit sheepish. They are half in and half out of costume, partly conventional, partly flamboyant. Under their chubby nipples they have painted clown faces; on either side of their paunches are false arms, clad in jackets and white gloves, which almost scrape the ground. They are, in effect, one and a half times the men they were. Behind them is a chap in full parade fig whose real phiz and upper parts are covered by a gigantic striped topper as long as his torso. The proportions are all to cock; it is as if everyone had been snapped in a distorting fairground mirror.

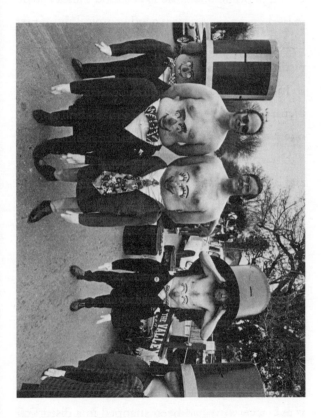

There is no message on the back of the card, just a greeting. 'Lots of love, Angie' is underscored with the wavy line which in the old days of marking up copy for printers was an instruction that the type should be in bold; Angela often used this wiggle to underline titles or her name on an article. The picture was its own message. Here was the America she relished, the country at its most unbuttoned, in carnival display. Here was that disconcerting mixture of the real and the fake, the natural and the manufactured to which Angela returned again and again.

She wrote about this mixture when she wrote about women and make-up, finding in black lipstick and red eyeshadow 'the cosmetic equivalent of Duchamp's moustache on the Mona Lisa ... cosmetics used as satire on cosmetics'; it could be heard in her conversational manner, which was at the same time artificial and gutsy. She spoke about it when I was asking her how she went about researching her novels. 'May I digress?' she asked, with a mandarin politeness that ruled out refusal. She did digress, swerving into a long and luscious description of a 'very very important' building from her childhood, the Granada cinema in Tooting. Angela knew how to use an emblem. The Granada's architecture mingled original and pastiche, the glorious and the kitsch; it was a building that both imposed and teased. As did her own work. Playing with style, making fairy tale and fantasy tell new truths, were at the root of her stories. When she dreamt up Fevvers in *Nights at the Circus* she produced a creature who was, as for a moment were Bill Owens' carnival men, rather more than human: an *aerialiste* who may or may not have had real wings pushing their way through her shoulder blades. Fevvers had as her slogan not 'Is she flesh or fowl?' but 'Is she fact or is she fiction?' That could also have been Angela's motto, both on the page and in life.

She liked to tell the story of how, when she was fifteen, her mother had found her reading a novel and had advised her to stop. 'She told me to remember what had happened to Madame Bovary.' Too good to be completely true, perhaps, but not quite as straightforward as it seems at first. Angela might not have shared her mother's anxiety about moral waywardness but she did think that romantic victimhood was worth combating, and she tackled it in her reimagining of fairy tales.

Her own reading tilted as much towards anthropology and philosophy as towards the novel. In her journals the writers she mentions – quoting and annotating them as if for scrutiny by an invisible tutor – include Sigmund Freud, Bertrand Russell, Barthes, Engels, Marx, Thomas Szasz, Lukács, Sartre, Marcuse, Frances Yates, Walter Benjamin, Louis Aragon, Nietzsche, de Sade, Novalis, de Rougemont, Melville, Adorno, Tzvetan Todorov. There they are, these bigwigs, alongside notes on *The Book of Clowns*, *A Dictionary of Angels*, the *American Heritage Cookbook*, *The History of the Harlequinade*, *The Haunted Screen*, *Wild Tigers and Tame Fleas*.

When *Wise Children* was about to appear in the summer of 1991, I asked her about the books that had been most important to her. She came up with her candidates without blinking. 'Nothing frivolous about my list, I'm afraid.' First was Dostoevsky's *The Idiot*. Then anything by Shakespeare, for 'brilliant enthusiasm for the work of Andrew Marvell: 'The combination of exquisite formalism and ideological correctness I find very attractive.' She asked that a poem by him should be read at her funeral.

Yet for her deepest admiration she went further back. Chaucer – who was 'so nice about women' and who, in the Wife of Bath, created a character she loved – was to her the 'sanest, the sweetest and most decent of English poets'. She liked the idea that he wrote 'before English became a language of imperialism'. She liked the notion that *The Canterbury Tales*, coming from an oral tradition, had to be direct and forceful enough to transmit when read aloud to a room full of people who were busy 'sewing or shelling peas'. She liked the aspects of Chaucer's work that pre-dated the novel, and half-disapproved of the genre in which she made her name. 'I'm sufficient of a doctrinaire to believe that the novel is the product of a leisured class. Actually.' That 'actually' dangling from the end of a sentence was habitual when she spoke. Dainty but adamant, it was like the flick of a heel or the toss of her head. It warded off objections but also invited contradiction. It both emphasised and slightly undermined what she had just said. Actually.

GEISHA

Geisha Boop arrived in my flat on a card in vivid Technicolor. The Betty Boop features – lidless eyes as round as coins and cheeks as fat as a mumps sufferer – squat between a fat hairstyle and a fan. Beside her, a hybrid animal in a kimono sits on a mat, strumming a samisen; in the background is a snow-capped peak.

The card, evidently sent in an envelope, is undated and unfranked but must have been dispatched in the late eighties. It is partly a work message: 'Forgive my narcissism, but I really do want somebody besides me & Lynn Knight at "Virago" to read this, & *you are the one*. If any Brontë stuff ever comes in, can I have it? *Nobody* has written about them properly, everything is crap.' Towards the end of her life she planned to put that right, by making a heroine of Jane Eyre's stepdaughter.

© 1987 King Features Syndicate, Inc./Fleischer Studios, Inc.

Her novel was to be called 'Adela: A Romance', and in 1991 she delivered an outline of the plot to Chatto. It was a piece of Angela's top-notch drollerie, a high-speed collision of the arch and the full-throttle, of literary allusion and bodice-ripper. It is hard to know whether this document would pass muster in today's publishing climate, more businesslike about the bottom line and used to sleekly presented proposals. Angela's 'advertisement' (she considered 'synopsis' too drab a word for the origins of a book) covered one side of a piece of A4 with her non-perfect typing, which sometimes mistook an 'i' for an 'e' or jammed two words together or missed a letter out: a touching aspect of looking at a typescript is that it registers the pressure of the writer's fingers. The novel explained what is suggested but not made certain in Charlotte Brontë's novel: that Mr Rochester's ward was actually his daughter. Adèle ('known as "Adela"') falls in love with her boarding-school headmistress, 'the aristocratic blue-stocking, Mrs T. who teaches her many things'. She determines to seduce her guardian, not knowing he is in fact her picture itself carries a memory of an earlier time: of Angela's first big excursion and her escape from England.

In 1969, when she had published three novels and been married to Paul Carter for some eight years, she won the Somerset Maugham Award for *Several Perceptions*. The award, given to a writer under thirty-five, was to be used for travel. Angela fulfilled that requirement, but gave it a twist: 'I used the money to run away from my husband, actually. I'm sure Somerset Maugham would have been very pleased.'

She ran to Japan, the only country that met her stringent criteria for a bolthole: she wanted to live in a non-Judaeo-Christian culture, but it had to be a culture with a good sewage and transport system. She was convinced that the world was ceasing to be Eurocentric: 'The Chinese and Japanese were snappy little imperialists when we were running around in woad.'

She lived for a time in a fishing village by the sea, then very pretty, later destroyed by a freeway, and she worked for a spell in the English language branch of NHK, Japan's government broadcaster. In 1972 she published *The Infernal Desire Machines of Doctor Hoffman*, 'the novel which marked the beginning of my obscurity. I went from being a very promising young writer to being completely ignored in two novels.' She took this dive in novelistic fortune as a sign that the sixties were at an end.

She had gone off with a Japanese man, a 'very good-looking bastard', in whom she found, looking to Revolutionary Russia and early French cinema for her reference points, a combination of Gallic Lothario and Russian nihilist: he had, she remembered, 'the face of Gérard Philipe and the soul of Nechayev'. The experience was, she claimed, 'very good, lovely, just what I needed after nine years of marriage', and it changed her. 'I became a feminist when I realised I could have been having all this instead of being married.' In Japan she became enthusiastic about sex. She found even the ads for the VD clinics jolly: 'Let me,' they cajoled, 'cure *your* chronic gonorrhoea.'

SIC

In 1988, four years before she died, Angela sent a bard card from Canada. A glossy black product of the Stratford Ontario Shakespeare Festival, it showed a cut-out of the playwright's face, high-domed and egg-like, resting on his ruff. The legend around him wildly signals facetiousness: in fluores-cent yellow, Neo-Renaissance Palatine italics and an exclamation mark, it proclaims: 'So I haven't writ-ten much lately! So what? Neither has Shakespeare.'

I cannot remember whether there was a partic-ular occasion for this card; the message on the back reports only that 'Canada's nice. Especially Montreal. Like Scandinavia with liquor.' What region of Scandinavia can she have been think-ing of? At the time she sent this card, Angela was dreaming up *Wise Children*, her last novel, and her Shakespeare book, a buoyant wise-cracker about hoofing and singing twins. The idea of writing about twins was part of her tribute to the drama-tist. She had been struck by a conversation between Iris Murdoch and A.S. Byatt in which Byatt had remarked that Shakespeare's influence on Murdoch

So I haven't written
much lately!
So what?
Neither has
Shakespeare

was apparent in the number of twins featured in her novels. Angela had set out intending to make some reference to all of his plays in *Wise Children*, but a few eluded her. Her favourite, *A Midsummer Night's Dream*, was resplendently there, 'a completely 20th-century great play', she thought it; what had been delicious fantasy for the Victorians was 'for us much more'. She replayed Lear's story twice, in male and female form; she planted two Falstaffs, one male and one female, and 'a positive welter of late comedies, including a whole lot of Calibans wearing penis sheaths', but she had not managed to get in *Titus Andronicus*, unless a ferocious cook counts as a reference to the Roman's frightful pie: 'Shakespeare's a bit of a vegetarian, good on fruit and veg, but rotten on meals,' she said.

Shakespeare was part of the yeast not only of her prose but of her plots. She read him 'like a novel', regarding *Measure for Measure* as 'a page-turner', and thought his stuff worked perfectly well without all that language: 'people weep and gnash their teeth over Ophelia in Peru'. She favoured the bland lines that moved the plot on: 'a ship has come from France'. She was dismissive of the routine idea that had he been alive now he would have been writing for television: he would more likely have been a used-car salesman.

Her Shakespeare card may also have been offering a semi-apology for a refusal to write something for the *London Review*, my attempts to coax her onto the page quite often met with refusals. She may have been wincing about the late delivery of a piece of copy. She liked the idea that journalism ran through her veins and was a terrific deadline surfer: 'the only time I ever iron the sheets or make meringues is when there is an absolutely urgent deadline in the offing'. Pieces had to be wheedled and winkled out of her during epic exchanges on the phone. 'I'm sorry I'm such a lousy deadline-keeper,' she wrote from London, enclosing a delayed review. 'But it's been the end of term & I had lots & lots of term-papers and I went deaf & I trod on a rabid squirrel & All has been Hell.' Still, in this Shakespeare card she was most likely nodding to the four years that had passed since the publication of *Nights at the*

Circus, the novel that had brought her a new blast of critical acclaim.

There was a good reason for the gap between Angela's books. In 1983 she had become pregnant. She was forty-two, mature for a first-time mother, and she was thrilled and alarmed: 'Alex came as a great surprise to us,' she told me.

Her pregnancy was not calm. She was not altogether well, and she did not take things easy. One of her tasks was the judging of the Booker Prize. It was the year that Fay Weldon presided over an unusually female-strong panel (Angela and Libby Purves sat in judgement alongside the literary editor Terence Kilmartin and the poet Peter Porter), and must have been an unsettling experience for Angela, whose own work had never been selected by a panel of judges.

It was to become even more unsettling. After the dinner at which the announcement of the winner (J. M. Coetzee's *Life and Times of Michael K*) had been made, the television presenter Selina Scott went around with her mike, smiling and making mistakes. She went up to Angela and apparently mistook her for one of the many hangers-on at the feast. She bent over her at the groaning board and inquired what she thought of the judges' decision. 'I'm one of the judges,' Angela explained, leaning away from her interrogator with a grimly polite chuckle. 'Does that exclude me . . .?' Poor Scott seemed mystified: 'I'm sorry . . . What's your name?'

The next morning the unrecognised novelist was whisked into hospital suffering from high blood pressure. Cards did not issue from the ward but letters did: 'Actually, it's perfectly okay in here, like a girl's dorm, & rather dreamy & soporific. The ante-natal ward is opposite the delivery rooms, so this sub-David Hamilton atmosphere – big, soft girls in nighties – is riven, occasionally, by the cries of the new-born . . .'

CHILI

In 1985 she sent me a postcard from Austin, Texas. The picture showed a black cauldron trying to pass as a saucepan. Bubbling with beans and frighteningly red beef, it was sending off a swirl of blue smoke; alongside it lay peppers, an open bottle of Lone Star beer – and a recipe for Texas Chili. Angela's message runs: 'Carter's reply to her critics! Texas chili, it goes through you like a dose of salts. I would like to forcefeed it to that drivelling wimp . . . preferably through his back passage. (I do think all that fuss was comic, though). Temperatures in the '80s. Everybody is loony, here.'

At the beginning of the year she had reviewed an assortment of volumes about food – *The Official Foodie Handbook*, Elizabeth David's *An Omelette and A Glass of Wine* and *The Chez Panisse Cookbook* – for the *London Review of Books*. In a sustained piece of invective, and a dextrous analysis of manners, she tore into 'piggery triumphant . . . [the] unashamed cult of conspicuous gluttony in the advanced industrialised countries, at just the time when Ethiopia is struck by a widely publicised famine'. It was not only the inequity and the waste that enraged her, it was also what she saw as the snobbery of that newly emerging species, the foodie. 'This mincing and finicking obsession with food opens up whole new areas of potential social shame. No wonder the British find it irresistible.' Furious responses – some of them alluding to the pregnancy which had delayed her piece – appeared on the paper's letters pages: 'A woman capable of splashing blame for the Ethiopian famine on Elizabeth David is scarcely to be trusted with a baby's pusher, let alone a stabbing knife.' They spoke of Angela's 'Puritanical contempt' and 'self-righteous priggery'. More than one took her to task for producing novels at all: 'many a serious scholar would consider the reading and creating of fiction a frivolous pastime'.

These critics were as wrong in thinking Angela uninterested in food as they were in misreading her to mean that foodies were actually responsible for famine. She did take pride in a certain austerity: she spoke of herself as having been formed by the 'mild discomfort' of England in the forties, the England of Stafford Cripps, and approved of its nourishing plainness, of 'the fact that you were always a litle bit healthily cold, and yet you had brown bread'. Yet austerity in her was the flipside of relish and gusto.

TEXAS RED and a LONG NECK*

TEXAS CHILI

2   tablespoons vegetable oil
2   pounds stewing beef, cubed
1   cup chopped onions
1   green bell pepper, seeded and chopped
1   clove garlic, minced
1   12 ounce can tomato paste
2½ cups water
2   pickled Jalapeno peppers,
    rinsed, seeded and chopped
1½ tablespoons chili powder
½   teaspoon crushed red pepper
½   teaspoon salt
½   teaspoon dried oregano
½   teaspoon cumin
1   15½ ounce can pinto beans, drained

In a large heavy pan, heat oil, and brown beef cubes on all sides. Add onions, bell pepper and garlic, and fry them with beef for about 5 minutes. Add all the remaining ingredients except beans, and simmer the chili for 1½ hours or until the meat is tender. Add beans, and simmer 30 minutes longer

* COURTESY OF LONE STAR BREWING CO., INC.

Angela, who talked more about her anthropological curiosity than about turns of phrase, was fiercely interested in the history of food and in its social implications. She injected not dislike or dismissiveness but quizzicalness into her review of the most sacred of culinary cows, Elizabeth David; in 1986 she filed a terrific piece about 'that godless vegetable' the potato. The book she had chosen for *Desert Island Discs* was *Larousse Gastronomique*: she wanted, she said, to take something that would be 'a good read'. Still, her interest was also practical, also personal. 'I'm a domestic person,' she declared. This was delivered with the assurance of someone who knew that the wild excursions of her novels and essays would never allow her to be thought of as a homebody: the description was something of a bluff, rather in the way that, she pointed out, Elizabeth David's 'deftness with the pans is not a sign of domesticity but of worldliness'. Like many of Angela's statements, this was accuracy parading itself as irony – and none the less ironic for that.

In the kitchen in Clapham she served up rabbit and broccoli, and lamb and apricots (the last cooked with a cat sitting on her lap). She was not much of a drinker; the first time I went to supper at 107 The Chase, I was dashed to see that as soon as the first glasses of white wine had been poured, the bottle was stoppered up and put back into the fridge. She had, she said, cooked 'endlessly, elaborately' during her first marriage, and claimed that, after they split up, her husband had accused her of having produced batches of wonderful cakes 'in order to make him fat and unattractive to other women. That was characteristic of my Machiavellian mind.'

Angela herself did not eat cakes. It was not apparent to most of her friends that, although she was a generous dolloper-out of food, her eating habits had been, for a large part of her life, irregular and sometimes dangerous. As a young girl she had been large, with a chubby face, and had reached her adult height of more than five foot eight by the time she was thirteen. At the age of eighteen she changed. She changed shape as dramatically as a creature in one of the fairy tales that fascinated her. She became anorexic.

She was clear about the reasons for this: she wanted to take control of her life and wrest her future away from her parents. Her father was 'fearless and unimaginative. I mistook his psychic good health for psychosis. I thought something must be desperately wrong because he was such a very adaptable and cheerful man.' Her mother, whom she described as coming from 'the examination-passing working classes', communicated to her daughter the feeling that if she was not going to go to Oxford or Cambridge she might as well not bother with higher education. Both parents were possessive, though in rather different ways; looking back on her adolescence, Angela thought of herself spending a large part of it entrenched in hostility towards them. Her mother indicated that if her daughter got a place at Oxford, she and her husband would be likely to get a flat or house nearby: 'I think, that's when I gave up working for my A levels,' Angela explained. And just after she'd taken her exams (only two of them), she gave up eating.

of the young, primly costumed Angela. 'I think this is very funny, but I'm not sure *why*,' runs her message. The black and white drawing shows a woman in a blouse with a Peter Pan collar and hair like an ornamental tea cosy. She is encased in her clothes, curved over and wary. The toe of one court shoe taps the ground; her tiny mouth is puckered; her button eyes are almost flying out of her stolid face with astonishment. The caption declares: 'Bambi's mother, reincarnated as a middle-aged divorcée, pawed the ground in her support hose and mid-height heels, quite bewildered in her new surroundings.'

The dainty fawn was on Angela's mind in the eighties. In 1985 she sent a card from Boston to her friend Edward Horesh: it showed Bambi on two legs holding a missile. It was entitled 'Bambo'.

Angela reckoned that as an acute condition her anorexia lasted for about two years, but in its chronic form it went on well into her mature life. Until she left home, until she split up with her first husband, there were many things she did not eat; right up to the birth of her son her eating patterns were 'still strange'. For some twenty years she levelled out

46

Bambi's mother, reincarnated as a middle-aged divorcée, pawed the ground in her support hose and mid-height heels, quite bewildered in her new surroundings.

at about sixty-three kilos but, after Alexander, she steadily put on weight. 'But I wasn't worried any more. I felt so much better when I was fatter. It made me think that inside every thin woman there's a fat woman trying to get out.' She went back to her pre-anorexic size.

LIKE A FLAMINGO

In 1986 Angela posted sunny sentences from Cedar Rapids, Iowa. 'I like it as much as I've liked anywhere in the States, including the French Quarter of New Orleans. (Though it's nothing like the French Quarter, of course). Everso rural; cornfields, and exquisite clean farms, like toys, and county roads white with dust. Al is starting to look like Huck Finn.'

This cracker-barrel cheeriness is given a sardonic twist by the picture on her card. Out of a lake of frozen sludge pokes the Statue of Liberty. You can see the spikes on her head, her drooping eyes and, alongside, the hand clasping the torch which looks dead; it would be hard to prove that she is sinking rather than emerging, but that's what it looks like.

The image was the creation of the Pail and Shovel Party, who in spring 1978 gained control of the student government at the University of Wisconsin-Madison. They pledged to arrange for all clocks on campus to run backwards, so that classes would finish before they had started, and they covered the lawn outside the administration building with a flock of 1,008 pink flamingos. The Liberty erection was their most famous feat: a forty-foot high replica made from papier mâché and chicken wire, which appeared on Lake Mendota in February 1979; the story was that the statue had been accidentally dropped from a helicopter.

Angela was at ease with such performance art and skilful at flipping between cosiness and wild surmise. It was a pattern established early on in her writing career. She had married at twenty-one; her husband, Paul, from whom she took her surname, was some eight years older and taught chemistry at what was then Bristol Technical College. Nearly thirty years later she could still patter off the routine of those years: 'Got up made breakfast sent husband off to work sat down and read the paper maybe did the crossword did a little light word-smithing.' House-smithing, light or otherwise, was not part of this scheme, so that when she later read Betty Friedan's call to pack in domestic chores and lay claim to a fuller life, it struck no chord: 'I never did any housework.' Instead, she dragged her husband to New Wave films and went to auctions with friends, accumulating heaps of furniture – 'people would come in and write 1789 in the dust' – and, as a birthday present for her husband, a bright red vintage vacuum cleaner. 'I hope he liked it.' She invested in what she claimed to be the larg-est collection of sardine tins in southern England; she liked the look of them and made, through her fascination with their design, a lifelong friend of a fellow enthusiast, the artist Corinna Sargood, who was to illustrate Angela's fairy tales with her swirl-ing lines and whorls and dark carnivalesque.

'Wilfully eccentric and whimsical' she called these times. But they marked the beginning of her political awakening. Her husband introduced her to 'big black blues singers and small white folk sing-ers' and Angela claimed that interviews for one

51

some relevance to what she was writing) a phallus-shaped head of Nosferatu; a label has been pasted in advising 'NEVER OPEN A WARM DOOR'. She published several poems in the Bristol University student paper *Nonesuch*, and others in little magazines of the kind that used to curl up together in the corners of bookshops; several appeared, rather surprisingly, in a literary quarterly sponsored by English Carmelites. One poem, 'The Magic Apple Tree', delivered with panache and a formal precision (the swipe of the last line is a terrific mimetic touch), is an early fierce fairy tale, an anteroom to *The Bloody Chamber*:

> The Queen, with 'ticing apples in her hand,
> Went out walking to see what she could see.
> 'Plump little boy, rosy little boy, come nearer.
> Here is an apple to do you good.
> Here is a basin to catch your blood.'
> She sticks him with a sharp knife
> Between the long ribs and the short.
> A necklace of beads, blood trinkling down,
> In the Queen's garden, where the apples grow.

Bud, blossom, bloom and bear,

Ready to tear,

So that we shall have apples and cider next year.

Hat-fulls, cap-fulls, three-bushel bag-fulls,

Little heaps under the stairs,

Cider running out of gutter-holes.

Hip, Hip, Hurrah!

Wipe the blade clean on the grass.

FLICKERINGS

From Taormina in 1987 she posted a picture of Etna exploding like a scarlet cock's crest, and a message full of delight. Angela loved Italian film – in fact, most film – and what she saw in Sicily could have come straight from the screen. Her sightings were buoyed up by her knowledge of old-time film stars: Rossano Brazzi had seduced his well-coiffed way through *South Pacific* and *Three Coins in the Fountain*. On the card she writes: 'Rosanno [sic] Brazzi (remember him) & his wife bring their poodle to dinner everyday in a shopping bag because dogs are not allowed on the hotel terrace. The other day a gift-wrapped Alfa Romeo was delivered to a pair of honeymooning newlyweds. Its fun. The boys are this moment in the sea, swimming. I sit on the terrace & contemplate my 3rd coffee.'

Up for 'anything that flickers', Angela had enjoyable brief encounters with celluloid during the eighties in *The Company of Wolves* and *The Magic Toyshop*. In the screenplays that languished unproduced in her filing cabinet, the literary tangoed with the explosively popular. A cowboy morality play, *Gun for the Devil*, paid tribute, in the name of the character Roxana, to Daniel Defoe. She plunged into Hollywood when in Albany, Upper New York State, toiling in the film section of the university and coming home laden with biographies 'with titles like "Too Late for Tears" or "Mascara in My Martini"'. Out of this research came great swathes of her last novel.

Wise Children was her London book, but also her film book and her fathers book. There is autobiography embedded here, though not of a literal kind. Dads and movies went together for Angela, whose

own father took her as a youngster to whatever was showing at the Granada, Tooting Bec. She was grateful that this led to her exposure to a host of 'unsuitable' films: the first she remembered, apart from *Snow White*, was *The Blue Lagoon*, which had Jean Simmons flat on her back on the sand to the sound of waves. Angela remembered herself as being six when she saw it, though she must have been nine.

It was not the movies alone that mattered in these excursions: the thirties super-cinema itself, 'one of the most beautiful, beautiful buildings in the world', was a dizzy delight and a revelation. A homage to the Alhambra, it had a Hall of Mirrors upstairs and a cyclorama, with the night sky projected on the ceiling of the upper gallery. It had a curved roof, huge murals, a marble staircase and amber mirrors. What transfixed Angela was its 'very, very difficult mix of real craftspersonship, real marble and fake marble . . . You never quite know what's what until you touch it. The stairs are real, fabulous marble, but the pillars are painted plaster.' As a child she 'took it for real. It's a masterpiece of kitsch, but in it was. 'We are back – just landed. I have strep. throat. Al has a streaming cold. Mark, with a grim face, is cleaning the oven; our tenants did not, not once during their tenancy. Thatcher has a four point lead in the polls. Christmas is but three days away. We go up north, to my brother, for this event – which I hope you will find bearable – but hope to see you soon afterwards. The Mid-West was lots of fun. Truly.'

She snarled and she frolicked: the combination made her strong meat. That and the full-out loquaciousness: few would argue that Angela's writing had an extensive acquaintance with litotes. After reading a contemporary's meticulously realistic work, she roared: 'There must be more to life than this.' In response to which, the novelist and critic Francis Wyndham raised his head from one of Angela's extravaganzas to murmur: 'There must be less to life than this.'

Taxed with overwriting, Angela ('I'm all for pretension') explained how eagerly she looked for opportunities to do so. 'Embrace them?' she retorted: 'I would say that I half-suffocate them

with the enthusiasm with which I wrap my arms and legs around them.' Dandyism and irony were, she declared, 'the weapons of the dispossessed'. They were not attributes that everyone welcomed. After her first success as a writer, the scholarly Henry Gifford declared that he wished she had studied some subject other than English.

Gifford, a mild-mannered but stringent Russian specialist, was professor of the English department at Bristol University, which Angela attended from 1962 to 1965. Her passage to university was not straightforward; nor was her time there particularly stimulating. Marriage had taken her to Bristol, where she applied for a job at the *Bristol Evening Post*, and was turned down. At a loose end and getting depressed, she was taken to lunch at Mario's Trattoria by her uncle Cecil. Her male relatives were always helpful: 'I guess that's why I'm more sympathetic to fathers than a lot of feminists.' Cecil suggested that university might stop her looking so peaky: 'If you've got a degree, you can always get a job. You can leave your husband any time you want.' She did not have enough A levels but the university 'didn't seem to mind at all'. She was in, but, as a mature student with a hubby, also slightly out; her social life – apart from one poet, one teacher and her lifelong friend Rebecca Howard – was based not among students but at home.

She was in any case sceptical of the idea that criticism in the arts was 'some sort of science'. She thought it was 'about taste – and it's about class, actually'. Towards the end of her life, she explained that she reared away 'in horror from the Leavisite construction of the sensitive reader ... I think of someone eczematic.' A few years earlier, when quarrels about literary theory were raging and cutting careers short in English departments, she wrote in spatting form from Providence: 'I've fallen among semioticians & am trying to make head or tail of the deconstructionists. I havn't [*sic*] got a dictionary in my flat & keep forgetting to look "hermeneutics" up in the library. It's been busy, busy, busy as far as thinking is concerned but I don't know how much use all this Dérrida [*sic*] and stuff is going to be when I get home. I keep wondering just what Dérrida is up to &, if he's so clever, why doesn't he write a novel of his own?'

Her time at university did leave her with an enduring attachment to medieval literature. She persisted in declaring that, despite the Wars of the Roses and the Black Death and the rise of anti-Semitism and other disadvantages, 'from the perspective of later history the medieval period looks like bliss'. Reading English also confirmed her fascination with the eighteenth century. She gave Robinson Crusoe a Beckettian makeover in one of her poems, setting him on a beach decorated with 'dandruff sand' and 'used contraceptives, slimey mementos'. She persuaded her tutor to let her write an essay on Defoe, fired up chiefly by the ringing, plausible voices he created for the heroines of *Roxana* and *Moll Flanders,* and spoke of Defoe's writing as a kind of Method acting, close to oral storytelling. The voice that nattered on and cajoled in fiction was the voice she cherished. It is this voice that inspires the narration of *Wise Children*. It is not a natural voice, this lor-luv-a-duck cockney with lashings of high-falutin' and of well read: the whole thing is a performance by performers, a mashed-together bit of impro. But it is unmistakably a spoken language.

FIBS

'A likely story,' Angela scoffs on the back of a card sent from Auckland in 1990. Its comic-strip picture – in early-movie lime-greens and violet-blues – was of a Maori legend, featuring the rivalry between a large fierce mountain with a glaring mask-like face, and a pacific brown rock: both were after the affections of a 'dainty' mound who looks like a heap of sugar. The consequences of their fall-out included a great fire and the creation of the Wanganui River.

There may be here a glancing reference to my enthusiasm for Bruce Chatwin, who had died the previous year. The book that had brought him most fame, *The Songlines*, had given glowing life to another Antipodean mythology, that of the Aborigines; it had also looped into free-wheeling speculation about primitive man and primeval beasts. Angela, born the same year as Bruce, with whom she had had a friendly encounter, had written warmly about the book but was sceptical about the far reaches of his anthropology. Bruce was looking for the origins of human instincts and belief; Angela's interest in folklore and myth was in the way it shaped and expressed individual psyches.

THE STORY of the MOUNTAINS

In the days of the gods, many mountains lived together beside Lake Taupo. The largest were Ruapehu, Taranaki (Egmont), Ngauruhoe and Tongariro.

Taranaki also loved Pihanga but Tongariro became angry and with great fire, drove Taranaki westwards.

Tongariro loved and married a dainty little mountain, Pihanga, who lived nearby.

As he fled he cut a deep channel, the Wanganui River, coming to rest by the sea where he remains.

A Maori Legend, New Zealand

In the last few years the lush and ferocious fables in *The Bloody Chamber* have been turned into a play by Northern Stage, an opera in San Francisco, and enacted by puppets as part of a Halloween show in Atlanta. These are the stories that most clearly proclaim Angela as a feminist writer with an agenda, or agender. Let us allow Bluebeard's last victim to be rescued not by a man but by her mother. Let us load the prose with red stains and howls, wet lips and shudders, and make evident what is buried in the stories we read to our children. Let us take the girls of traditional fairy tale and give them some force of character: on *Woman's Hour*, Angela pointed out that it would be hard to argue that the Sleeping Beauty was 'a figure full of get up and go'.

The chilly landscape of these stories may, she thought, have come about because they were written in Sheffield, where she had gone on an Arts Council scholarship. She arrived there in the mid-seventies and so just missed William Empson, who had retired as Professor of English Literature in 1971. Like Angela, Empson was a high-wire stylist, an atheist and an admirer of Andrew Marvell;

like her, he had lived in Japan. They met later when Angela went to hear him lecturing – her with her flyaway hair, him with the slipping-down beard that he wore round his neck like a bib – but all Angela reported to me about the critical illuminator of ambiguity was that he made (not for her) a seduction drink from tinned raspberries and condensed milk.

There were other reasons for that frozen landscape. As a child she had read not only Andrew Lang's fairy tales but also the stories of the nineteenth-century minister George MacDonald. MacDonald, a friend of Lewis Carroll, Tennyson and Wilkie Collins, came, as did Angela's father, from Aberdeenshire and embodied a 'Northern European rational romanticism that I admire very much'. She consumed his work so avidly and in such great quantities that when she started reading Norwegian and Gallic stories for her Virago collections of fairy tales, she experienced something 'very, very atavistic . . . I felt this genuine shudder inside me as though I'd heard these stories before I was born.'

The other kind of story that ran in her blood was journalistic. Her father had worked for the Press Association: she described him as talking in the 'stately prose of a 1930s *Times* leader' scattered with period phrases: a bitter day was 'cold, bleak, gloomy and glum, Cold as the hairs on a polar bear's bum'. It was he who when she left school at eighteen got her taken on at the *Croydon Advertiser*, where she found in the newsdesk 'a great source of baroque character', invented a record-review column and was quickly marked down as a feature writer rather than a news hound: 'I had a demonic inaccuracy.' She also hit on a small but significant feature of her later journalism. She began using the first person – in places that person did not usually reach – as a way of making sure she got a byline: her gambit was to use 'I' so often that a sub-editor couldn't be bothered to keep taking it out, and had to put her name on the piece. It was also a feminist device: she decided early on that men often avoided using the first person in order to acquire a bit of gravitas.

Angela found her strength as a journalist in the late sixties, urged on by Paul Barker at *New*

Society. She wrote about *Playgirl*'s men, Bradford chimneys and fetishistic fabrics. She wrote about 'fine-boned, blue-eyed English madness in Bath', Japanese tattooing and Habitat. During my twelve years on the editorial staff of the *London Review of Books*, hers was the copy I was keenest to read. She was the only reviewer who could deliver with equal pungency on the ANC and on Colette, and who could tell us that D. H. Lawrence was 'a stocking man, not a leg man'. With her full-throated admiration, her scorn, her learning and her fearlessness, she made her reviews into enduring essays.

VILE

At the end of 1987 she sent Christmas and New Year wishes from her and Mark and 'a very spotty Alex – he's just come down with chicken pox'. The card had two sets of red line drawings: a 'For Her' section showed a couple of jewel-encrusted rings, a sports car and a speedboat; the 'For Him' section was strewn with plaid slippers, a stag, a pair of binoculars and a crown. Actually, *the* Crown. The picture shows tinted photographs of Prince Charles and Lady Diana back to back under the headline 'All I want for Christmas is . . .' Diana's answer is 'A divorce'; Charles's clenched-jaw response runs: 'I wasn't thinking of anything that expensive.'

The royal family afforded Angela the pleasure of rolling-eyed ridicule. She liked to put it about that the Queen had a secret black love-child, claiming that you could see the gleam in the monarch's eye when she was surrounded by Commonwealth heads of state. Angela would have manned the barricades at a revolution but she kept her vitriol for those who were politically active. A birthday card – bearing her instruction to open 'wide, but carefully' – showed her enlisting royal support against a greater grisliness. The picture on the front displays the Queen, in full tasselled, ermined regalia, with Windsor Castle in the background and a speech bubble floating over a plush curtain: 'I see London, I see France . . .' On sliding open, the panels making up the royal image re-form to reveal the then PM, in purple bra, orange boxers (with football motif), high-heeled pom-pom mules and a string of pearls.

She is hoovering in front of the telly; above her a gloating comment rhymes with the one overleaf: 'I see Maggie in her UNDERPANTS!'

It is hard to exaggerate the visceral anti-Thatcherism of the eighties. The complaints, often focusing on Thatcher's voice, were tainted with misogyny (has any vehement male politician ever been accused of shrillness?); often they were polluted with snobbery (Thatcher sounded 'suburban'). Angela never held back on abuse of politicians; at the time of the outbreak of the Gulf War the message she left on my answering machine was simply a string of oaths. She did not hold back about Thatcher: 'I think that no fate is too vile for her,' she said after the introduction of an internal market in the National Health Service. Yet her real political anxiety was wide-reaching, and prescient: 'The worst things are probably things we don't know about. They're to do with surveillance and they're to do with the Secret Service, and they're to do with the inaccessibility of information . . . I imagine that this has been a period of such incredible overwhelming public corruption that it will take years and years before we know about it.'

BLISS

From New South Wales came two versions of Utopia. One on each side of a card. 'What *really* fascinates me about Australia,' she wrote, 'besides the flowers & birds & trees & exquisite mammals – is this: it's the stage on which the great drama of the British working class is played out on a hugely magnified scale. That's my pet theory of the moment, anyway.' Actually, it was a pretty settled theory, to which she returned when I interviewed her for the *Independent on Sunday* in 1991. Australia was, she declared, 'the most beautiful country I've ever seen and the despised and the rejected have inherited it and . . . after a couple of generations they turn out to be six foot tall, incredibly good-looking, smart and republican. I think it's terrific.' She saw Britain becoming 'visibly less egalitarian all the time' and Australia inspired her. It showed 'what America was invented for'; why could Poms not do as Aussies did, and be civil without being servile? When I asked if she wanted to write about the Australian novelist Christina Stead, her response was unequivocally enthusiastic, though her description would not beguile everyone: 'I think she's wonderful, by Dostoevsky out of Brecht.' Her piece, which appeared in the autumn of 1982, spoke with ardour of Stead's importance: 'We have grown accustomed to the idea that we live in pygmy times.' Angela's own unpygmy-sized theory about fiction was: 'It is possible to be a great novelist – that is, to render a veracious account of your times – and a bad writer – that is, an incompetent practitioner of applied linguistics.'

Her postcard eulogy to the Antipodes ended on a domestic note: 'We are fine. Alex has grown,' and the picture on the other side was a maternal romance, an apolitical Eden. The Australian artist E. Phillips Fox painted *On the Beach* in 1909: the picture belongs to the lifetime but not the sensibility of Angela's grandmother, whom she compared to St Pancras station and who kept three copies of Foxe's *Book of Martyrs* in her house. By the side of a green-blue sea, boaters and tucked-up skirts and lacy parasols are dawdling; in the water, sailor suits and high-necked swimming costumes join hands. In the foreground stands a woman with a

E. Phillips Fox, *Bathing Hour* (*L'heure du bain*) c. 1909 © Queensland Art Gallery

copper-coloured bun and an empire-line white dress. She is towelling the arm of a small bare girl whose bottom, feet and tilted cheek are glowing red, as if she were standing by a hearth.

Angela said she believed more and more that 'our lives are all about our childhoods'. She spoke of herself as having been a podgy little girl, of having wanted at the age of eight to be an Egyptologist, of having been 'a lot of people's second-best friend' at her 'really bad' direct-grant girls' grammar school in Streatham. She spoke of Alexander with astonished pleasure. His arrival also meant the beginning of a new era of concern. She knew that 'as long as I lived I wouldn't cease to be anxious', and cited a moment in the Royal Festival Hall when seven-year-old Alex had for seconds disappeared behind a shelf of records: 'My heart stopped.'

I asked her during my interview to describe Mark. 'Big and fierce,' she said. 'So MALE,' she said with admiration to her friend and agent Deborah Rogers. Angela sheltered under his silence and supposed ferocity: 'My co-habitant is very frightening,' she explained, when Mark arrived to collect her from a Fontana party: she tiptoed away, as if mocking her own meekness – but with alacrity. Alexander was a dreamer and was becoming a word-sharpener. He invented a game called Killer Baby, and, in the cabin of a narrow boat, which his parents kept moored in Camden, told a long and intricate story about a mouse. The creature had caught a cold. A very bad cold. A cold that invited a pause for horror. A very very bad cold. Then it had caught something worse. It had caught. Extremely long pause. 'A taxi.' Something of Angela's had been transmitted here: she always made sure when I, who, like her, did not drive, arrived at The Chase, that I knew the times of the last buses home so that I would not have to shell out for a cab.

The sight of the three of them in their narrow boat was striking. Heading to Ladbroke Grove to pick up groceries from Sainsbury's, they slipped past the backs of London streets as if they were part of the city's subconscious. Mark was at the tiller, tall and bearded; Alexander was inside playing. Angela sat at the window, waving like the Queen.

CATS

They were her familiars, the mogs. Angela did not sent me cards featuring felines, but she made a point (she knew her friends) of sending them to her friend and publisher Carmen Callil, a cat lover who names her pets after loved ones, sometimes to disconcerting effect (is it Angela's great friend and agent Deborah Rogers who has distemper or Carmen's border terrier?). Carmen got a card of a puss with evilly bared teeth and one of two cats playing chess. While being berated for her attack on foodies in the *London Review of Books*, Angela sent a card to Carmen to tell her 'I seem to have won the James Tait Black prize – or at least half of it.' (J. G. Ballard got the other half.) The picture showed a cat in tux and bow tie giving his order to a feline waiter: 'I'll have the chocolate mouse.' Angela's PS explained: 'Thought I might send this card to Susannah as my reply to the abuse with which I have been heaped in L.R.B.'

Ponce and Female – Female being the mother of Ponce, who lived off his mum – were Angela's own cats. They had been very present in the house, but spent more time in the garden once Alexander, 'with his father's eyes and his mother's short fuse', began to crawl around the kitchen. Carmen chose for the cover of Angela's dramatic works a gorgeously coloured crayon picture by the author, which showed black cats with huge triangular eyes advancing in a gang over what looks like the floor of 107 The Chase.

Her first book, written at the age of six, was called 'Tom Cat Goes to Market'; her mother kept it for some time, then threw it out. In 1979 she wrote a text for the artist Martin Leman's *Comic and Curious Cats* and in 1982 a sex-driven version of *Puss in Boots*. Towards the end of her life *The Sea Cat*, a feline tale for children, in particular Alexander, combined the comfort of an ugly-duckling story with the disconcerting image of a moggie who was at home not just in the water but under it. That secret life of cats – both fluffy and feral – intrigued her; she wrote two of her best poems about them. In one of them, 'Life-Affirming Poem about Small Pregnant White Cat', the creature is a 'bulging sack

SPLATTERED

'All DAMNED!' Angela signed off a missive from Austin, Texas, where she was working at the university in the mid-eighties. Her card was a photograph of an armadillo, a curved creature picking its dainty way, like an elderly millionairess, through prickly undergrowth; her message, which let the picture float like a tantalising emblem, flashed from close-focus to apocalypse. 'The armadillo,' she wrote, 'is the hedgehog of Texas. You see them splattered over roads. First it snowed; then it rained; then it froze. Now the sun shines. How long will it last? ... No international news gets through at all; *what about the miners*? ... this is Boom Town, U.S.A, fairly discreet money – all aerospace industry. All DAMNED!'

The United States brought out with torrential force her feeling that the capitalist world was going to hell in a handbasket. Not that there was ever any mystery about her political views. For all her magnificent humour, Angela was never frightened of coming on as socialist and solemn. She had less fear of the Brechtian placard than any writer

I have met, and no one would have much difficulty in deducing her political views from her fiction; she believed that 'a narrative is an argument stated in fictional terms'. Still, for most of the time her fiction did not state her subversions but embodied them, not only when she was clearly remaking the female mythology of fairy tale but also when she unpicked the fabric of first-person narration. What she did in *Wise Children* was fundamental and bold: she put the reins of her story into the hands of a working-class woman who tells it colloquially and with eloquence; she is not patronised – or matronised – by authorial comment. The same cannot be said of more obviously observant Leftist writers, and Angela came in for some stick from some of the sisters for being an Uncle Tom. Discussing 'real novels' – the sort in which 'people drink tea and commit adultery' – she wrote: 'If a comic charlady obtrudes upon the action of a real novel, I will fling the novel against the wall amidst a flood of obscenities because the presence of such a character tells me more than I wish to know about the way her creator sees the world.'

In her correspondence – as in her journalism – she shot straight: no metaphors, no obliquity and much literal reproduction of conversations. There was also tremendous bileful opinion: a meek inquiry about the progress of a review would be met with vivid, sometimes violent political paragraphs.

From Providence, Rhode Island, in 1980, Angela reported: 'Most people take it for granted Reagan will get in.' I thought at the time that she must have got this wrong, or gone loopy. 'Everybody tells me not to go out after dark; the Mayor of Providence is [accused of having] raped a woman at gunpoint, admittedly some years ago in another town.'

A little later in the year she used her political disgust as one of her excuses for failing to file some copy: 'I was overcome with wild, weary anger at the spectacle of the criminals, psychotics & retards whom Reagan has appointed to man the ship of the States & could not lend my mind to Sloane Rangers. No, truly. I've been contemplating Last Things in the frozen solitude of the New England winter & I couldn't think of anything insightful to say about Ray Gosling & the other bloke except that they are really rather alike, which isn't a very interesting thing to say, since the same culture produced them.'

In Providence she mused: 'I briefly contemplated joining the Communist Party on my return to the U.K. Then I thought, while I was here, I'd join the American C.P. & see if they tried to extradite me. Then I fell into a state of sullen & terrified apathy. (I may join the I.M.G., if this goes on.)' She felt her seething made her foreign. In Providence, 'ordinary people are so decent & kind – &, as for blacks, they've cut their own throats by being decent & kind. One of my students gave me a story in which the narrator goes to London & takes a taxi in from Heathrow & the taxi-driver says to him: "That'll be fifteen bleedin' quid, you miserable wanker." How did this upper-class Eastern seaboard American child capture the exact speech rhythms of the British working class? It made me weep with nostalgia for the sheer rudeness – the vile, obscene, funny *rudeness* – of everyday life at home. Certainly Europeans tolerate & probably actively enjoy a degree of verbal abuse amongst themselves that would be unimagineable here. Here, *physical* violence is tolerated. The crime rates would go right down, I think, if Americans stopped saying: "Have a nice day," to one another. At least it would stop *me* from contemplating violence; when people in shops & so on order me to have a nice day in this authoritarian way, I want to kill, kill, kill. When I mutter "sod off" under my breath, they think it is a Russian Orthodox benediction.'

BUM

The bum arrived in the post over twenty years ago. Angela always liked a bit of rude. Bawdy – as in pantomime, or the Wife of Bath – was a kind of rude she particularly favoured. In her twenties, and a lover of the Scots Chaucerians, she produced a salty version of William Dunbar's 'Tua Mariit Wemen and the Wedo':

> 'I'm tied to a shadow, a worm, a blind old
>   man so shagged out he can't do anything
>   but talk. He's nothing but a bagfull of snot.

86

He can't even keep his trousers clean. He's
    always
Scratching himself, scratching everywhere,
No shame.
It's disgusting.
I could burst into tears when he kisses me.
His five o'clock shadow bristles like pig-hide
    (but it's
The only thing about him that can stand up to
    attention, if you get my meaning).

She would also go along with kitsch naughtiness, as in the card sent from Le Beausset in the Var, franked 4 August 1990. At first glance they look like rocks, two substantial mounds set in a purpling blue sea. But the drops of water on the slopes are too pearly, and the slopes themselves too luxuriantly yielding to be stone. They are another of Angela's now-you-see-it-now-you-don't *trompe-l'œil*, parts of a semi-submerged body, jauntily captioned in pink lettering: 'Qu'est-ce qu'on est bien dans l'eau! . . .' Angela's message is simply: 'lots of love, Angie, Mark & Alex. XXX'

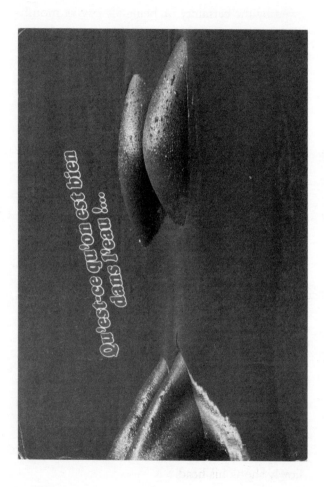

Qu'est-ce qu'on est bien
dans l'eau !...

The card was sent in the last year of good health, or, rather, the last year in which she was not shadowed by the certainty of being ill. Twelve months later, when that shadow hovered around everything, Carmen invited Angela, Mark, Alexander and me to stay with her in the South of France. It was hot; Alex played in the swimming pool; a bat got into the room where Mark and Angela were sleeping, and scared her; Angela drew with her bright crayons. Two photographs, taken during a supper by the side of the Canal du Midi, now seem charged, by a trick of the light, with a threatening intensity: the faces around the table swim out of an almost pitch-black background. Alex, looking like a star, is throwing out a wide and radiant beam; Angela – in specs and a black dress, her hair catching the light like a beacon – is smiling gently; Mark looks troubled. One afternoon during our stay we started to talk about exploring the region at different times of the year. Carmen and I said we'd like to come back in the spring; Angela joined in enthusiastically. But, sitting behind her, Mark slowly shook his head.

For much of those last two years, when I saw Angela, her vitality still held. She was forthright, not elegiac; she cursed rather than complained; her feminism and socialism did not waver. Speaking up for sex rather than romance was a thread in this vitality. 'Say what you like about Catholicism,' she threw out, 'they do think married couples ought to have sex.' She held it against Britain and Protestantism that one idea of a happy marriage could be (she slipped in a reference to Virginia and Leonard Woolf) a chaste liaison. And she despised the idea that 'now that women have got their men in the kitchen, doing the washing-up, making meals, now they've got them in the nursery changing nappies, they don't like them any more . . . they can't get off on them.' Her own view was altogether different: 'I find *nothing* more erotic than the spectacle of a man up to his elbows in the sink.'

TWIN PEAKS

Conjoined cherubs dimpled on the invitation to the *Wise Children* party on 12 June 1991. They were the only picture on the card; in those days, publishing invitations were plain affairs. The putti were Chatto's colophon, but they could have been a sly reference to the heroines of Angela's book. She had based Nora and Dora Chance on the Dolly Sisters. The Hungarian-born twins were famous for their vaudeville dancing acts (they appeared on stage as candied fruit and, with a troupe of performing dogs, as 'The Dollies with their Collies'), their gambling, and their lovers: one of them had Gordon Selfridge in thrall, a fact on which Angela, whose mother had worked as a cashier in Selfridges, was particularly keen.

Writing about their rambunctious days was one way of restoring the life of Angela's aunt Kit. The pre-war London of *Wise Children*, 'a city of casual glamour, off-hand, rather masculine', had been enjoyed by Angela's mother, 'a Socialist who liked a nice frock', but it had made Kit miserable. When she failed her exams, her parents thought she might 'go on the Halls' but she was pushed by a prim headmistress into a job as a 'clerkess' in Victoria Street. In the war she took to wandering the streets during the blackout: she 'adored seeing those flying bombs'. She died in Tooting Mental Hospital. *Wise Children* showed the giddy time she might have had. It did so by putting her into a theatrical dynasty, which Angela told me she had based on the Redgrave family.

'It's nearly killed me,' she said of *Wise Children*. 'It's taken me ages to do this book. I had this deep conviction that when I'd finished something awful would happen.' Yet, 'What a joy it is to dance and sing!' proclaims Dora Chance, and the book was published with much hoofing delight. Chatto made posters of the Dollies with plumes on their heads and stiff gauze skirts sprouting from their waists. They also put together a tape. The music on it expressed the heart of the book and much of its author: 'Brush up your Shakespeare' from *Kiss Me Kate*, Ivor Novello's 'Rose of England', 'Is You Is Or Is You Ain't My Baby', Kathleen Ferrier singing 'Che Faro', 'My Heart Belongs to Daddy', 'I Can't Give You Anything But Love, Baby', 'The Moon Shines Bright on Charlie Chaplin', Fred Astaire crooning 'Let's Face the Music and Dance'. At the party in Carmen's Ladbroke Grove house,

Angela sat on the sofa with Mark at her side and received a stream of guests. Yes, she said, unusually fulsome, when I said she must feel pleased by the packed room and the plaudits, 'I feel loved.' Chatto's Jonathan Burnham played the piano. Francis Wyndham sang 'If You Were the Only Girl in the World'. The hostess ended the musical turns with 'The Red Flag'.

Wise Children was written in what Angela regarded as an era of London fiction. Martin Amis had published *London Fields* three years earlier; Michael Moorcock's *Mother London* had appeared in 1988; Iain Sinclair was beginning to expand his mystic sociology and East End explorations, and Angela reviewed *Downriver* in the *London Review of Books*. The city was, she thought, being biographised just as it was being irrevocably altered, torn down and its history wiped out. The Lord Morrison pub in Lambeth had had the Low cartoon of London taken off its sign and been renamed Stockers Wine Bar; the Ernest Bevin School in Tooting might have its name changed 'maybe not to Michael Heseltine but to Twin Peaks or Four Seasons'. All wrong, on her bed. Back at home, with Mark at the front door warding off people who took it into their heads to drop in, she entertained. I remember her, in October 1991, angry because the Labour Party had rung her on the day she came out of hospital to badger her about a fund-raising dinner; she had recently been asked by the *Evening Standard* why she supported Labour: 'Well,' she said, 'the Labour Party, it's like an old sofa, you go on sitting on it even if it is Kinnock-stained.' She was thin, then, and wore a red ribbon wound around her head and tied in a bow. While Mark cooked pasta, Alexander read a children's encyclopaedia that had been sent by the *Guardian*. Angela claimed the literary editor had taken a poll of reviewers and that she had come out as 'the most deserving'; she enjoyed explaining that a first copy had been sent with '£100 worth of books' stamped on the parcel, and had been swiped.

In the midst of her treatment, she concocted a riposte to the Booker, which expressed her comic contempt for much of the fiction flying around the place. Once more missing from the shortlist for the prize, she had, she noted, failed to get the sympathy surrounding trees rearranged themselves. They shifted and they sprouted feet. They marched and dispelled, shaking themselves free of foliage. They changed into Special Branch men, who were moving forward to enclose the author of *Midnight's Children*, in hiding because of the fatwa imposed on him by the Ayatollah Khomeini three years earlier. The previous year, when Angela was working on the strongly secular television documentary *The Holy Family Album*, Rushdie had offered her advice on how to deal with blasphemy. 'I don't think,' she had gleefully retorted, 'I need any help from *you*.'

The memorial service, held some five weeks later, was as expansive, inclusive and gaudy as the funeral had been small, plain and sober. Corinna Sargood created a shocking-pink invitation. Not exactly a postcard, but a card certainly, covered in curling black drawings. This was a miniature work of art, by a friend who had been in tune with Angela since they had met in a Bristol shop when they were in their twenties. The card folded over on itself from both ends, its outside flaps were drawn with swagged curtains, gathered at their tops in rosettes, and it opened like a small theatrical event onto its invitation. Two Ionian pillars, on either side of which hovered a wheeling owl and a parrot, contained an onstage menagerie; in front of a row of footlights, on bare boards, were a giraffe and a peacock, a dive-bombing swallow and a leering goose. A pair of workmen's boots were climbing a ladder; a paintbrush was waving; there was a spade, a bucket, a crescent moon, a shooting star and a hand holding out from the wings a glass of bubbling-over champagne.

The invitation was to celebrate Angela's life and works at the Ritzy cinema in Brixton at 11 a.m. on Sunday 29 March. The Granada Tooting had been the obvious choice for the event – which Angela would surely not have wanted called a service, or a memorial – but that cinema had become a bingo hall. It was Mark who came up with the idea of the Ritzy. It was a homage to Angela's love of the flicks; the hoofing heroines of her last novel would have felt at home there; it was splendid but battered, and had nothing super or American about it; it was in south London, where she had made her home.

The morning was based on *Desert Island Discs*. Angela had been asked to go on the programme towards the end of her life: she had chosen her eight records, the book she would take and her luxury, but she was never recorded. She claimed that Radio 4 had decided to bring forward the transmission of the Prime Minister John Major's programme and put off the date of her recording; she was then too ill to get to a studio.

At a quarter to ten on 29 March a front-of-house man was doing his best to sweep up the rubbish between the seats at the Ritzy, while keeping an eye on his toddler daughter who staggered around with a dummy in her mouth. A collection for the Brompton Hospital raised over six hundred pounds; Alexander held out a bucket.

Michael Berkeley, composer, broadcaster and friend, was the compère in the crammed and dusty place. He sat on a podium with a cassette machine in front of a folding screen, which Corinna had painted with tropical verdure. He announced the tapes and summoned up the speakers: people from different parts and times of Angela's life stood in for her voice. Carmen, wearing her koala bear jumper ('for Angie'), spoke, as she had at the funeral. Rebecca Howard talked; so did Caryl Phillips. Tariq Ali fired off about the miners' strike and made Salman Rushdie cross when he called the Ritzy a fleapit. Lorna Sage arrived just before the morning kicked off: she was pale, slightly stooped and breathless. She, too, was to die in her fifties, but her long blonde hair streamed down as if she were a nineteen-year-old.

For her records, Angela had chosen Debussy's 'The Girl with the Flaxen Hair', because Hugh had played it when he was a music student, and Muddy Waters' 'Mannish Boy' because it brought back the fifties. She wanted an extract from Schumann's *Dichterliebe*, sung by Dietrich Fischer-Dieskau, because it was the first LP she ever bought, and Billie Holiday – her voice shot through with crackles and sighs – singing 'Willow Weep', because it reminded her of Streatham Ice Rink. She asked for Sviatoslav Richter playing Schubert's B flat Piano Sonata, which she described as her favourite piece of music; in one of our last meetings she had said she now preferred Schubert to Beethoven – 'more heart'. Woody Guthrie's 'Riding in My Car' she chose because she liked being driven and because it reminded her of being in the car with Alexander, who was learning it on his guitar. The penultimate number was Bob Marley's 'No Woman No Cry': played at an unfamiliar speed, it wound through the place like treacle. On the tape decks was David Miller, at the time Deborah Rogers' assistant. He was beckoned to an aisle seat by one of Rushdie's bodyguards. 'You're playing this at the wrong speed,' said Rushdie. But weird and slow though it was, this was the recording that Angela had in her collection, so Miller stuck to his guns. As the song wound slowly on, the actress and writer Pauline Melville stood up from her seat and began to dance. The author of short stories about shape-shifting rolled her shoulders and hips very gradually; she looked like a graceful hallucination. The final record was one of Richard Strauss's 'Four Last Songs'; Hugh said that was something on which she would never have alighted had she not been ill. In the middle of it, a poster of *Wise Children* which had been stuck up at one side of the stage came loose and fluttered down.

When the time came for Angela's luxury to be announced, Mark and Alexander came up from the audience and onto the stage. They turned around Corinna's bright screen. On the back of the scene of island vegetation she had painted Angela's choice of luxury. It was a zebra.

ACKNOWLEDGEMENTS

I would not have written any book without the early encouragement of Christopher Ricks and Karl Miller. I would not have written this book without the prompting of my friends Tim Dee, of BBC Radio, and Alexandra Pringle, of Bloomsbury.

I am grateful to Mark Pearce, Alexander Pearce and Rose Boyt, and to Lindsay Duguid and Carol McDaid from whose terrific editorial advice I have greatly benefited.

Thanks, also, to Edward Horesh, Rebecca Howard and Corinna Sargood, to Xandra Bingley,

Michael Holroyd, Fiona Maddocks, Diana Melly, Rick Stroud and Francis Wyndham; to my agent David Miller and, at Bloomsbury, to Holly MacDonald, Paul Nash, Anya Rosenberg, Anna Simpson, Justine Taylor and Alexa von Hirschberg. Thanks to the Authors' Foundation.

I owe a particular debt of gratitude to my friends Georgina Brown, Anne Chisholm, Richard Hollis and Posy Simmonds.